The Joy of Booking

The Joy of Booking

a guide to buying and selling used SF books

by **Bud Webster**

The Merry Blacksmith Press

2011

The Joy of Booking:
A Guide to Buying and Selling Used SF Books

© 2011 Bud Webster

For information, address:

The Merry Blacksmith Press
70 Lenox Ave.
West Warwick, RI 02893

merryblacksmith.com

Cover by Bob Snare

Published in the USA by The Merry Blacksmith Press

ISBN—0615523439
978-0615523439

Dedication:

To the memory and honor of Vince Gilligan and Nelson Bond, antiquarian bookmen *extraordinaires*: if I'm able to pass along even a tenth of the knowledge they've given me, I'll consider it a job well done.

Table of Contents

Preface

It behooves me, right up front, to make it clear what we're going to cover in the *The Joy of Booking*'s coming pages—and, even more important, what we aren't going to cover. Not to mention my qualifications for doing this in the first place. Off and on, I've been selling used sf and fantasy books for the past 35-plus years, at conventions, through the mail, and more recently, online. Not *once* in all that time have I owned, operated, or worked in a brick & mortar used bookshop, although I have from time to time consulted for a few.

Any advice and suggestions I have to give here are directed *not* at those of you who want to open retail storefronts, but at the part-time seller who's looking to supplement his/her income, to help defray the expense of adding to his/her own collections, or simply to find a way to help cover the travel and hotel expenses of going to the conventions he/she would be going to anyway.

Foreword

bib·li·o·phile: (bi-blē-ə-ˌfī(-ə)l) also **bib·li·o·phil** (-fil) or
bib·li·oph·i·list (-əst), *n.*

      1. A lover of books.

      2. A collector of books.

                (From www.thefreedictionary.com)

That covers it reasonably well, I think. You can't be one without the other, you know, and if you're reading this, then we all know that you're both, poor thing.

(There's a third aspect of this, of course, which is the focus of this particular treatise, and which is almost certainly the primary *raison d'être* for your having purchased it in the first place, but we'll get to that soon enough.)

My life-long love of the bound codex is evident to any and/or all who venture into my general environment. There are books in every room; stored neatly on shelves, stacked carefully on tables, painstakingly packed in boxes and bags and piled precariously on nearly every flat surface in the joint.

I come by it honestly. My folks taught me to read at a very early age, and I was surrounded by books as a kid. One in particular was to have a significant affect on me on several levels: *The World's Best Loved Poems*, edited by James Gilchrist Lawson for Harper in 1927. About half of it was made up of "inspirational" or "newspaper" verse, which are interesting at this point primarily as artifacts of the time; but it also contained Shakespeare, Poe, Whitman and Robert W. Service, who are still among my favorites.

My sisters, ten years older than I, had school books from their English classes that I devoured as soon as I could hold them. Reading quickly became my favorite sport, replacing dodge-ball at which I excelled. Not. When I was issued my own English Lit books, I ran through them the first week—I may not have been a straight-A student, but I knew those stories and poems long before the teacher "taught" them to us.

I only had a small bookcase in my room as a kid, and its contents ebbed and flowed weekly as I checked books out of the library, read them, and returned them to get more. This regularity endeared me to the very kind ladies at the public library; so much, in fact, that I was given an extremely special dispensation one afternoon.

I do not recall the circumstances under which this occurred, in all honesty. I may very well have been told, or heard about it on the news, but somehow in the early 1960s the main branch of the Roanoke, Virginia, Public Library was tapped to house—however briefly—a copy of the Gutenberg Bible. Even while in elementary school, I understood how important this book was. I suspect, thinking back on it now, that it had been the subject of an announcement in English class (or possibly at my church one Sunday), but however word came to me, come to me it did.

I don't know how long that magnificent relic stayed in town; it may have been a few days or a week as it awaited transportation to another lucky library, but I know it wasn't a permanent addition to their holdings. I don't recall now, almost a half-century later, if I asked about it or if I was invited by a librarian to view it. What I do recall, though…

I recall walking downstairs to the library's vault, cool and still. I recall the librarian opening the cage with a ring of keys that made a sound I'd never before heard, an overture of sorts to an opera of truly biblical proportions. I recall her pulling on a pair of white cotton gloves, walking me softly into the vault, speaking to me in quiet tones; I have no idea what her religious views were, and frankly, they were then and are now totally irrelevant, as her adoration was almost certainly more for the object in front of us than for its spiritual importance.

She solemnly cautioned me not to touch it, so I put my hands behind my back as I padded into the cage behind her, anticipation making my heart beat faster and widening my eyes so as not to miss a single aspect of this marvel, this relic of more than just sacred consequence.

And there it was. My eyes filled with the sheer enormity of it; I could smell the leather binding and the vellum pages; the very creaking of that binding and the music the pages made as she slowly and gently turned them rang in my ears in a way nothing else had, ever before. I was more than captivated, I was ensorcelled. The age of it, the dignity and brilliance it represented fill me with a reverence that had little to do with the scriptures it contained.

I knew—I *knew*—deep in my innards that here was the single object that had made it possible for me to read about Tom Corbett, and Charlotte and Wilbur, and Alice and the Mad Hatter, and Mrs. Whatsit, and Huck and Tom, and the wonderful mushroom planet, and the Cat in the Hat, and Toad of Toad Hall, and and and....

Those of us who read (and write) science-fiction and fantasy are well-acquainted with the true sixth sense, that of Wonder. I thought I'd known Wonder before that afternoon in that cool, silent basement, but I'd only known wonder. That day I came face to face with it in its fully-capitalized form, a book made by a man who'd been gone from the skin of this planet for more than twice the number of years America had even existed. It was 307mm by 447mm, 1,275 pages long, forty-two lines to a page in double columns.

It was *huge*. Even now it looms, overshadowing all the other books I've owned—hell, even *seen*—establishing a benchmark along my personal bibliographic highway that no flood or fire can ever destroy. It inspired awe in me that I haven't felt since, and (at this point in my life) never expect to feel again. My British friends have a word for it: gob-smacked.

Happily, I've never quite recovered from that experience; I treasure it, in fact. It stirred in me an even greater respect and affection for books than I already had then, a bibliophilia that transcended the contents and spilled over into the Thing Itself.

"But, Bud," I hear you cry in confusion. "However can you bear to part with those books that you claim to love so much, and for mere money?"

Well, hoss, I'll tell you: it ain't always easy. I've sold books that I later regretted letting go of; I think we all have. Sometimes I needed the money, but all too often it was out of sheer ignorance. No excuse.

There's this, though. What you love, you love to share. You know how, when you get a new Whatever It Is You Collect, you can't wait to get it home so you can make phone calls, send e-mails, post about it on MyFace? So what if you found *two* of those Whatevers for the same price? Or bought a whole boxful at a yard-sale for $5?

eBay, am I right? Hey, that way, all those spoons (or Hummels or commemorative plates or Beanie Babies or pogs—remember pogs?) will pay for themselves, and your Spouse will stop tapping his/her feet and looking so cranky about it all.

I love books, I love the very idea of them, and I share them all the time. I give some away (those too rough to sell, or for which I have no buyers); I trade some in for others I can sell; I even sell a few to the bag-boys at my local grocery store. The rest I take to conventions and sell to my customers, old and new, who are looking for something to read and cherish.

I am a bibliophile. I'll bet you are, too.

1

Who Sells Books?

There comes a time in the affairs of many readers, especially readers of genre fiction, when they realize that they've somehow accumulated any number of books in which they have little or no interest.

This happens because they've habitually hit all the local flea-markets and yard sales for the past few years in a determined attempt to nail down that last book in their favorite tetralogy, and therefore bought books by the boxful. Or they've inherited all the books their friends were finished with.

Since their local used bookshop only gives a quarter of the cover price in trade regardless of the scarcity of the books, they figure to make back some of the bucks they've spent since 1974 by trying to sell those six Gor paperbacks (or that book club edition of *Lord Foul's Bane* or that run of *FATE* magazine from the early '50s) to somebody who not only *wants* them but is willing to pay a reasonable price.

Of such circumstances are avocational booksellers born[1].

Bookselling is a rarified (you should excuse the pun) area in which to operate, especially in the case of used and rare books. It takes a certain kind of person to be happy doing it: it's dusty, moldy, dark, and people look at you funny and ask when you're going to get a *real* job.

There's a significant amount of time and effort involved simply in becoming familiar with the lore and minutiae of edition points, terminology, areas of specialization, and history as well. If you don't like to do research, this isn't the hobby for you, because you'll spend hours poring over old catalogs, consulting web sites, making phone calls to book-folk more knowledgeable than you, and finding all the reference works you need to do your job properly.

And understand, please, that there is *absolutely* no substitute for learning the ropes, however you do it. It takes time and effort and not a little outlay of capital to turn yourself into almost any kind of bookman short of one simply flogging two-for-one romance novels out of a storefront or off a flea-market table. Just as you'd have to learn the correct techniques for painting fantasy miniatures, or how to assemble a top preparatory to quilting it, you have to learn the tools of your trade. And, the more specialized you become, the more lore there is, but we're going to assume that you like what you're doing to begin with and that this will be far less onerous than if you didn't.

Still want to be bookseller? Go through the prozines and look for ads from used booksellers. Send 'em a couple of bucks (or whatever they ask) for a copy of their latest sales list or catalog. File them away after you've looked them over, and refer to them frequently in preparing your own lists. There are many booksellers who've been around for years and have firmly established reputations for accuracy and fairness, such as Lloyd Currey, Barry Levin, Graham Holroyd, Pandora's Books, and many others. There are addresses at the end of this book, and I suggest you write each one and ask to be placed on their mailing lists. Don't hesitate to send them a few bucks to cover printing and mailing, as many of them will refund this on your first order.

Online references can be iffy, because there are any number of know-nothings out there and they have the same access to the web that real booksellers have, and their websites look just as good.

Your best resource, in my opinion, is AddAll.com, which searches not only Abe Books, Half.Com and Powell's, but more than a dozen other such services in the US and abroad, and will present search results from all of them sorted pretty much any way you want it. The full URL is http://www.used.addall.com, and I find I use it on a daily basis when I'm pricing stock.

Perhaps more important than either of these is the cultivation of a good, solid relationship with another, more experienced, bookseller. In many cases, a quick call to someone with a better reference library or just a headful of more facts can make all the difference. Choose wisely, though, and keep your questions to a minimum; their time is worth something, too, and they have their own business to attend to.

One prerequisite to being successful as a bookseller—as an avocation or otherwise—is a good, solid love of books, not only for what they contain, but as artifacts in their own right. If you'd be as happy selling vinyl siding or double-glazed windows, then do that instead. Do *not* clutter an already crowded profession with just another yobbo who wants to get rich. (Oh, and by the way, you won't. Get rich, that is. Not even maybe. As a hobbyist, you can supplement your income, support your own collecting habit, and maybe take the wife/the husband/the kids/whomever out to dinner once in a while, *after* you've replaced your stock and spent the time and energy inventorying it. As a full-timer, you *might—MIGHT*—be able to keep a bookshop afloat without going out of business in six months. Lloyd Currey and Barry Levin are the exceptions, not the baseline.)

Vince Gilligan, rest his soul, owner and operator of the Richmond Bookshop for decades and a bookman who taught me an enormous amount about selling books, made it very clear to me one time: "Bud," he said, "you can collect, or you can be a bookseller. Don't try to be both at once."

He was right; for all that I'm certain that he had his own shelffull of obscure titles. I know I do. If you can't stand to let something go, think twice about buying it for stock. I've lost track of the books I've sold and later regretted having done so. I don't doubt for a minute that *every* bookseller out there has similar regrets. I think it's unavoidable, but why set yourself up for heartache? Decide where the line is, and don't let it move. Much.

Why Sell Books?

Because, although there is no such thing as "too many books," the concept of "not enough shelf space" is all too common. Eventually, your wife/husband/ life-partner is going to make you get rid of them, so you might as well expend a little effort and fell two ornithomorphs with one projectile by a.) ridding the house of those pesky unwanted books; and b.) making a little money in the process.

Also, you like books, right? You almost certainly have a collection, whether it's signed first editions or tattered paperbacks, and you are only too familiar with remarks like "Have you really read all of these?" and "Are all of these your books?" and, worst of all, "Heh-heh. Gee, I wish I still had time to read, but these days I'm just *too busy.*"

Conversely, if you collected ceramic owls or thimbles or commemorative spoons, you'd probably be reading a little book on those rather than on books, so let's just go with the assumption that a.) you like books; and b.) you'd like to try and sell some, for whatever reason. So the impetus to acquire and handle (hell, fondle!) books is there, we just have to direct it.

There's another reason to sell books, one that's a lot more subtle and hard to quantify than simply wanting to free some space in the living room. There's a real sense of pride in selling a fine book, whether it's an old Avon Merritt with the laminate still intact and the colors bright, or an Arkham House first with a Lee

Brown Coye jacket covered in Mylar looking as it did when it was first offered.

A good book can be a masterwork of the binder's craft; a great book can be art. You aren't just passing along the words, you're enriching someone else's life—and making money at the same time.

When a customer comes to me at my table, list in hand and asking about something for which he's been searching for years, then finds it and two others he didn't even know about, I feel an excitement and a pride that hasn't diminished in thirty years. I don't think it will any time in the next thirty, either. Filling that hole on his bookshelf, providing him with the pleasure of completing a collection or just selling him an afternoon's read is something that fulfills me in a way that nothing else ever has. That he's happy to pay me for the privilege is icing on the cake—but it's mighty tasty icing, and I'm not so altruistic that I prefer my cake plain.

So, we sell books because we love them.

What To Sell?

Well, there's no simple answer to this, but you can start with books you have duplicates of, then go on to the ones you've read and don't intend to re-read, add the ones you bought fully intending to read seven years ago and have never gotten around to, and then just the ones you no longer care about.

If you're honest with yourself, and are taking this seriously, you've probably got a pile of 100-150 books right now without even breaking a sweat. Later on, we'll look into how you can acquire even more.

You'll want to decide on your limitations, too: how much space you have to store inventory, for example, might determine whether you go with hard and soft bindings, or just paperbacks.

Who are your favorite authors? Pick up lots of extra copies of their books, because your interest in them will help you sell those titles to someone else. Enthusiasm is contagious. On the other hand, an author you *don't* care for will still sell; there's a reason they make that ice cream with three flavors in one box, and as long as you don't actively discourage a buyer from buying that awful series by J. Boring Windbag, the fact that the books are there to be bought makes it possible that they *will* be.

Also, decide if you're going to specialize or flog whatever comes to hand. This is especially important when you're traveling to another state to set up in a big room with a dozen other merchants.

If you're behind a table at a mystery con, does it make much sense to take history books? Or heavy art books? No, you just take mysteries, with a smattering of books in other genres by mystery authors. Specializing makes it easier for you to reach a target audience, one already predisposed to spend money on that particular subject. It makes it easier to choose stock, which can be a real time-saver—I spend enough time in bookshops just looking through the sf/fantasy. If I went through the whole place I'd have to pack a lunch. And dinner. Your time is worth something, so don't sell yourself short.

I sell what I sell because I have the knowledge it takes to do so at least reasonably well. When you collect something, it behooves you to know as much as possible about it so that you don't miss out on something obscure and, more importantly, you don't get ripped off, right? I've spent three decades learning as much as I can about sf and fantasy books, and in acquiring a reference library that will enable me to continue to learn, so why not make a buck off that knowledge?

Paperbacks

I look for classic sf and fantasy mass-market paperbacks, in good shape (as good as I can find, in fact) as my primary stock. Why classic? Because that's what I know best, and therefore that's what I can sell the easiest. You'll hear me use the phrase "hand-sell" from time to time, and what this means is that I don't just display my inventory, I make suggestions to potential customers based on what they've asked me for. If they've asked me for Delany, I'll suggest Philip K. Dick; if they ask for Fred Pohl, I'll mention Kornbluth. I do carry a few newer authors, mostly hard-science writers like Catherine Asaro and the Benford/Brin/Bear Axis, but my concentration is on the books I grew up reading.

There are specific authors and titles that I always want to have in stock, and I keep a list that I can pass on to the local two-for-ones so they can keep an eye out for them. I do daily searches on eBay for new auctions featuring those authors, so that if someone offers a dozen Heinlein books, or a stack of anthologies, or something else I know I can sell, I can decide whether or not to bid. Mostly I don't; buying individual books is a mug's game if you're a dealer unless it's something very, very special.

When it *is* something very, very special (like the original Dell "Universe" chapbook by Heinlein), I'll put it on my watch list and refrain from bidding unless the opening bid is super cheap. Since I check every day, I don't miss out on much I'm actually interested in. Overall, I've been lucky more often than I've been unlucky.

Good condition, low price (do not forget to figure shipping into your cost), salability; these are the primary elements that help determine what paperbacks I buy.

I also try very hard to find fine copies of paperback originals, and I price them accordingly. There's a very eager market for old paperbacks in fine nick, and fewer and fewer of them to be found these days. You can get a premium price for many of them, depending on the author and publisher, but understand that just because it looks sound doesn't mean the spine won't split down the middle first time your buyer opens it. Price accordingly; you owe it to them.

Trade Paperbacks

In recent years, a number of small presses (like Wildside and the publisher of this book, Merry Blacksmith) have used print-on-demand technology to reprint older material in trade-paper format. This is, by and large, a good thing as long as the binding is done well, and the covers are attractive. Many of the authors I can sell well in mass-market are now available in trade-paper, brand new with no stains. I don't go out of my way to find them, but I certainly don't pass them up when they come my way. Readers love them, and that's your principal customer base.

Hardcovers

Again, classic titles by past masters of the field, preferably in the first edition with complete jackets. Better than reading copies, but not necessarily collectors' editions, these are offered for the buyer who wants something nicer/more impressive than a paperback. Be particular in what you buy for stock, however, because they not only take up more space (both on your table and at home) but weigh more, and on Sunday afternoon at the end of a long weekend, that's a consideration.

If you can find a good deal on collectors' editions at an estate auction, or from an old friend, then by all means bring them along. Don't be too disappointed if they don't sell if you're at a smaller con, though. I might take them if the author is a guest, but otherwise it can be too much trouble for my purposes. At a larger con, or a WorldCon, by all means knock yourself out.

What I do find profitable are many of the hardcovers sold by the Science Fiction Book Club, believe it or not. They tend to be sneered at by the cognoscenti, but many of them are excellent choices for the clientele I have.

For example, the SFBC has done a number of "combined editions," single volumes that comprise two or more novels in one binding such as Asimov's *Foundation Trilogy*, van Vogt's *Triad* (which combines *Slan*, *The World of Null-A*, and *The Voyage of the Space Beagle*), as well as the two-volume *Chronicles of Amber*, which collects the first five of Zelazny's Amber novels.

In addition, in many cases the SFBC is the only readily available hardcover edition of a title. The SF Hall of Fame books, edited by Robert Silverberg and Ben Bova, are almost impossible to find in a trade edition as is the equally important two-volume *A Treasury of Great Science Fiction* edited by Anthony Boucher. The afore-mentioned Zelazny set includes the first Amber novel, *Nine Princes in Amber*, a book that regularly sells in the mid-four figures in the first edition; for a reader who wants a copy in hardcover but isn't a high-pocket collector, the book club set is the way to go.

Some high-dollar novels have managed to become so sought after that they've dragged their book club counterparts up with them. *Gateway* by Frederik Pohl, for example, sells for far less than its big brother; nevertheless, it changes hands for more than the few dollars it originally cost club members and would still be worth under other circumstances.

There are a few SFBC titles that actually are the first editions. One example, unique in my experience, is Harlan Ellison's *The Beast That Shouted Love at the Heart of the World*. The original Avon paperback as issued in 1969 was heavily edited by an over-ambitious copy editor who presumed she knew better than Ellison how his stories should have been written. When the Science Fiction Book Club brought out their version a year or so later, Ellison had restored those stories to their original state. Thus, although the paperback remains the *true* first edition, the book club issue is considered the *correct* first. Under most circumstances, this sort of thing is important only to the rabid collector (like me), but here, with the very text of the stories at stake, it's of more than just bibliographic concern.

Other book club firsts include the volume one of Stephen Donaldson's first Thomas Covenant trilogy (*Lord Foul's Bane*, which I mentioned earlier), and most of the "Best Of..." series published by Ballantine in the mid to late 1970s. These are well worth having for stock anyway, as they really do represent the best works of their titular authors, are frequently edited by other well-known writers/editors and, in one or two cases, include introductions or afterwords by the authors themselves. Keep an eye out for them in either format, as they're perpetual sellers.

4

Where To Sell?

Let's assume for the sake of simplicity that we're talking about genre titles: sf, fantasy, horror and any other related books, since this will give us a baseline from which we can work, and also give you a few more options than a more generalized stock. Keeping in mind that we're not talking here about brick-and-mortar shops, you have three primary choices: science fiction and genre conventions, mail-order, and online. There are a few other avenues to sell books, but since we want to stay within the boundaries of the simplest solution, we'll ignore them for the time being.

Conventions

The advantages of selling at conventions are 1.) you can meet and interact with your customers; and 2.) your customers can handle and inspect your stock. Both of these are vitally important. When selling face-to-face, you get to work your salesmanship magic on them, and they can see exactly what they're getting. You're not only dealing with a captive audience, but one which is already predisposed to buy what you're selling. The disadvantage is that it can be much more expensive than the other two options, what with travel/hotel/table expenses, food, and the time it takes from your no-doubt already busy life. Plus, you've got to lug great heavy boxes of books out to your car, into the dealers' room, set them up on display, then reverse the whole thing in a couple of days. This can be an onerous task, unless you have help—and if you want help, better bring it with you—and unless you get there early for the con, you can miss sales by not being ready when the room opens to the public.

But what if you would have gone to the con anyhow? This affects your time outlay, and to a certain extent your expenses; your investment, depending on table cost, can, in many cases, be recouped by the time the dealers' room closes Friday night. I can honestly say that in the past six years that I've been selling cheap sf/fantasy paperbacks at cons, I've never yet failed to make all my expenses—tables, room, food, and travel, and even at the worst, I've made a profit—even if it was only $100 or so. And, as you'll see later on, I've taken steps to make loading, set-up and break-down quicker and easier.

The Book Geek convention case. Note that my name is written on the top in permanent silver marker. The name is enough to identify it as mine at cons, so my address stays private. Photo by Bob Snare.

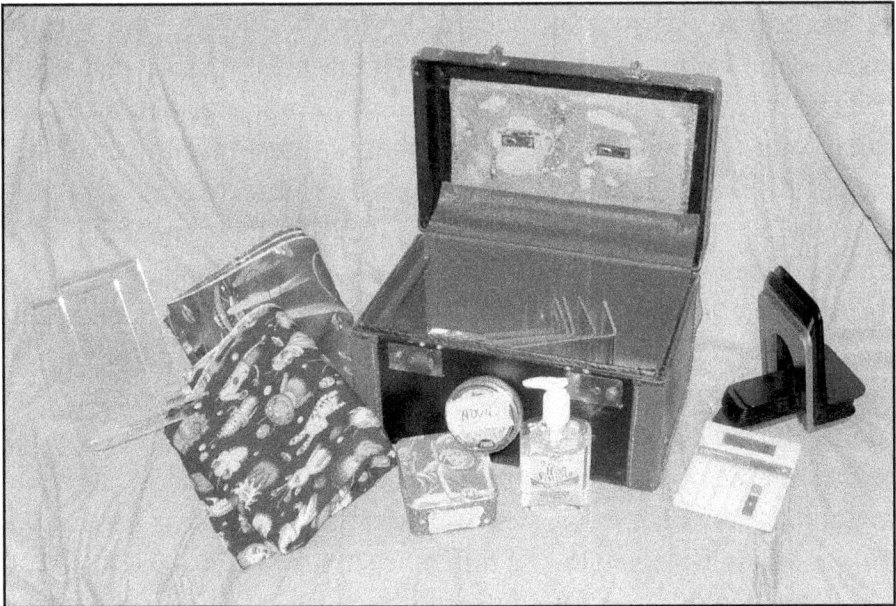

Left to right: book easels, table covers, money box, aspirin tin, hand sanitizer, calculator, and bookends. More easels inside. I know the case looks sad, but if you were that old and beat-up, so would you. Photo by Bob Snare.

How much money can you realistically expect to make? Well, there are a number of factors to consider. How big is the con? Where is it? What's your stock? What kind of con is it? Obviously, taking Gnome Press firsts to a small gaming convention in a little college town is no way to make a living. By the same token, almost anything you take to a major regional or WorldCon is going to sell, but your expenses are going to be a lot higher than usual (unless you live in the city where the con is, or have relatives there), so bringing $2 reader paperbacks might be a waste of space. A good rule of thumb is to choose your stock by your expenses—at a small con, take the cheap stuff; at a WorldCon, break out the Big Boys. Oh, and bring something to cover the table. The covers the hotel supplies don't always cover the whole thing. I'll give you a short list of things to carry along with you later on in the book.[2]

Setting up and taking down are aspects of traveling shows that have to be dealt with, as they tend to be the most labor intensive and time-consuming parts of selling at conventions. You not only have to decide how to display your books, but how best to combine display with transportation. Most booksellers I know use bookshelves, usually collapsible ones, which they have to unload, put together, and then stock before the room opens to the public. Others use some sort of table-top display, with any excess overstock kept underneath in boxes.

My own personal method is based around long, shallow plastic storage boxes with tight-fitting lids. With some foam spacers added in the bottom, they hold two rows of standard mass-market paperbacks, about 70-80 books per box. The books are in alphabetical order and the box lids are numbered, so all I have to do is wheel them into the room, put the boxes on the tables, pop the lids off, and I'm open for business. Max time from first to last: five to ten minutes,[3] so I'm ready to go when my competitors are still sweating to get their shelves up. This speedy set-up can make a difference in how your weekend goes.

Take-down is just as simple and fast; for one thing, when the other guys are busy dismantling their displays on Sunday afternoon, you can still be open and selling.

Mail-Order Catalogs

The second way to flog books is the most traditional of the three: put together a catalog, assemble (or acquire) a mailing list, and get it in the mail. Follow it up with another, different catalog in six months or so. The advantages are obvious: no travel, no box lugging, and no hotel/gas/food bills.

The disadvantages include the time and effort necessary to put a catalog together (I'm presuming you already have appropriate stock ready to list), and the long and frequently frustrating task of assembling a mailing list.

You can, as many other dealers have in the past, take a spot ad in *Locus* or one of the fiction magazines, advertising that you're preparing a catalog of sf books and inviting readers to send their addresses plus maybe a buck or two to help you defray the cost of printing and mailing the catalog. If you do, consider giving them back that dollar as a discount on their first order.

Or, if you have a good relationship with another mail-order bookseller, you might ask if you can use their mailing list, but don't expect too much charity; successful booksellers have invested a lot of time and money in assembling their list of customers, and they guard them jealously. This is leaving aside for the moment the question of whether their customers even *want* to be on another list—and they may very well not.

Once you have a decent mailing list (30-40 names isn't a bad place to start, although you want to add as many more as you can as you go along) and a serviceable catalog,[4] investigate what it will cost to print it. If you have only a few pages and stay at standard paper size (8.5 x 11 in.), you can staple at the upper left corner and save the cost of binding. If you have more than a few pages, print two-up in landscape format (whatever you're using as a word processor can set this up) so that the pages are consecutive, and then ask the copy-shop to collate and saddle-bind it. This will cost more, but if you've assembled a 32-page catalog, you'll need to consider this seriously. And make sure you shop around for prices; Kinko's isn't always the best place to go for this.

The downside of catalog sales is that your customers have to trust that you know what you're talking about, and that you aren't being deliberately misleading. There's no easy way around this, either. You have to build a reputation over a period of years, with satisfied customers who are willing to pass along your catalog to someone else (who will hopefully sign up to be added to your mailing list) or to vouch for you to potential buyers.

Customer satisfaction means one thing in this context: if they don't like the book, for any reason, you take it back and give them a full refund. No hedging, no argument, no weaseling. It doesn't even matter if you're right and they're wrong. If they aren't satisfied, you do whatever it takes to make them so[5]. Another downside is packing and shipping. This is time consuming, especially if you do it right, and there's absolutely no point in doing it any other way. We'll get into the correct way to pack later on, but we can tackle shipping here.

Shipping methods should be left up to the buyer. Which way you go depends on what they're willing to pay: USPS or UPS, Media Rate or Next Day, insured or not; these have different costs and requirements according to the carrier. Some buyers are comfortable with the Postal Service, others insist on UPS. If you aren't willing to do both, make it as clear as you can in your catalog which you intend to use, and the costs.

In fact, *everything* should be spelled out in the first pages of your catalog. Mailing address (snail- and e-), preferred methods of payment, name to which a check should be made, shipping instructions; all of that should be right up front.

This serves two purposes. First, it tells the buyer what they can expect, and second, it gives you a clear statement to which you can point in case of a disagreement about what the statement covers. You'd be surprised how many people will jump on a book they've been looking for years, and never read the "fine print" that tells them how to make out the money order.

Decide what, if any, handling charge you're going to add, and please don't be ridiculous about it. Charging a $6.95 handling fee for a $3 book is simply ludicrous, but I see it all the time. Author and antiquarian bookman Nelson Bond made it easy: Since he'd never been able to figure out a way to pack a book *without* handling it, he didn't charge for it. Makes perfect sense to me.

Although I don't charge a "handling" fee, I will round up the total of book price and postage to the nearest dollar; this extra quarter or half-buck helps defray the cost of those packing materials I have to buy. I try to recycle everything, but you always end up having to buy bubble-wrap or mailers. Think of it as the Cost of Doing Business, a concept I'll return to anon.

I should point out here that although a printed catalog sent through the USPS is one of the most traditional ways to advertise and sell books, it is, in this day and age, something of an anachronism. After all, why go to the expense of listing, formatting, printing and/or binding, and stamping? Why not simply set up a webpage?

Good question, I'm glad I asked. Here's the answer: people who like books like printed paper. Duh, right? Go ahead and spend a little money and have a copy shop print out your catalog, complete with ordering info and descriptions, just as I've instructed above. Lead off the first page with the URL for your webpage, which you have previously set up with the same listings complete with scans or photos, and send it out. Keep a stack of extra copies to hand out to customers at conventions, or that book group you go to every month, or the kids behind the deli counter who've been buying your duplicate Vonnegut and Leiber paperbacks. I mean what the hell, right? Cost of Doing You-Know-What. Your predecessors in Antiquarian Book Asgard will beam down on you and shower you with dust and paper flakes.

Online Listings and Auctions

Third, and in some ways most important, is selling online, either through a listing service like ABE, or with an online auction service like eBay. This option is important if for no other reason than that you have access to buyers *all over the world*, not just the ones in the room or on a mailing list. Thousands, if not tens of thousands of potential customers scour the online listings and auction sites every day. Some are looking for specific items; some just want to browse.

Every single one of them will buy from you if you give them what they want. Of course, in reality it isn't that easy. You don't just have competition from the other bookseller across the room or the four used bookshops in your town. You're competing with several thousand booksellers all over the world, and they're just as hungry as you are, if not hungrier.

Your primary advantage is plain—you have the kind of exposure that advertising agencies pay millions of dollars for. Your primary disadvantage, though, is the other side of that coin; there are 75 other copies of your book listed, and some of them are cheaper than you can afford to sell yours for. There's really no way around this. It's the marketplace in action.

All you can do is be scrupulously fair in your descriptions, keep your costs (and therefore, your prices) as low as you can, and make sure that your bibliographic information is as dead-on correct as you can make it.

I can't stress that enough. I see people selling books online everyday who might as well be running a yard sale for all they know about books. They don't know the nomenclature, they don't know edition points, and they can't tell a book-club edition from a slip-cased limited if you put a gun to their head.

Yet they will *try* to use bookseller words and terminology, and they invariably screw it up, leading not only to problems with the specific title they've misrepresented, but making it harder and harder for real booksellers to gain the trust of a thrice-or-more burned customer base. That's right; you're going to have to run as fast as you can just to stay in one place, all because of the yobbos out there who can't tell a first edition from the First Lady.

So, you do the best research you can, you learn the proper terminology, and if you ain't sure of the points, *just say so*. It's far better to look a little uninformed than it is to look dishonest. Or worse, to look stooopid. "Uninformed" can be fixed, "stooopid" is forever.

Here's a suggestion, one I cannot stress highly enough. If you list books on eBay—and with all its flaws and annoying fees it's still a darned good place to sell books—please, please, *please* do not fail to include a photo or scan of the cover, and make certain it accurately represents the book(s) you're offering. More about this later.

The Cost of Doing Business (CoDB)

I want to pay particular attention to this concept, as it can have a tremendous effect on the avocational bookseller. The cost of doing business is something with which everyone who does business of any kind anywhere in the world has to deal sooner or later. It's as unavoidable as April 15th, but can be far easier to handle. Put at its most basic, it comes to this: how much of a free ride does your customer get?

Break it down. What does it cost in time and money to buy, store, list, pack and ship a book? Ideally, as little as possible, but we live in the real world where these things can be slippery. Obviously, when you're talking about used books, this is going to be different for each one, at least as far as your purchase cost is concerned, but that is your basic CoDB. How much you add to that cost can determine your success or failure.

For example, as I mentioned above, I don't charge a handling fee for shipping books, although I do charge for postage unless the price is so high that I can swallow that cost and not choke. I do round up the total of book and postage to the next whole dollar amount to help pay for materials, but that frequently comes to 25¢ or less, and is useful only in the aggregate, assuming I sell enough. When a customer bids over a certain amount on a book, I insure it on my nickel. I spend reasonable amount of time and effort packing books securely, which would qualify as "handling" with almost any other seller, but as I tend to do this while sitting in front of the TV late at night watching old sf flicks, it's of little consequence to me; I'd be there anyhow, it keeps me busy, and since it takes place outside the general working day, it doesn't take that time away from much of anything else I'd be doing except annoying the cats.

So, that is *my* Cost of Doing Business, which means that my customers tend to get a little more of a free ride than someone else's do. I can afford it, but a seller who has to pay an assistant or who otherwise can't afford the time out of their day may not. You have to decide on your own, based on your level of commitment and the amount of free time you have to devote to it. (Please note that I haven't said a word about federal, state, and/or local taxes; they certainly enter into it, but there just ain't no way I'm going to offer any advice on taxes except to strongly urge you to consult an accountant or tax attorney.)

5

When To Sell?

Retail is cyclic. Always has been, always will be. Some months are good, some are bad, and knowing which is which can make a big difference in whether or not you show a profit. Obviously, your best months are going to be those leading up to Christmas. Even after the holiday, there's a brief period in which those who got gift certificates or cash spend them with wild abandon, and if you're there with the goods, they'll toss some of it your way.

After Christmas, the bills come due, and for a couple of months you won't be able to sell water to a Martian sand-rat. (Conversely, this can be the best time to buy—no competition in the auctions, and shop owners will frequently discount heavily if you buy in bulk.)

Things will pick up then, but come summer you'll hit another dead spot while people are on vacation. Then *those* bills come due, but in general they aren't as bad as the post-Christmas ones.

This is as true online as it is in the dealers' rooms, and if you're smart, you'll hold back on the heavy hitters until the boom periods; there's no sense in getting $15 for that Gnome Press first edition when you can get $75 for it in a few months.

Aside from that, go for it. Keep a weekly listing of something on eBay so you can establish a track record (and hopefully pile up the positive feedback—which, as flawed a system as it might be, is all your bidders have to go by), salting it with occasional nice pieces to keep the big spenders interested in looking at everything you have. If you're worried about those nice pieces not bringing in good bids, set the reserve high or make the opening bid more than $10. Idle bidders looking for bargains will pass by on their way to cheaper stuff, and you'll more than likely still have the book to offer in times of plenty.

How To Sell

Aye, there's the rub. Salesmanship is not an easy concept to describe; it's a complex of attitudes and talents. You don't have to wear bow ties or checked pants, and you certainly don't have to mislead a potential customer just to get them to test drive someone else's old clinker.

First and foremost, you have to be able to communicate well. You have to hold your customer's attention and direct it to the item you're trying to sell him, and engage him to the point where he forgets that you're trying to get him to open his wallet, if only for a few seconds.

Sincerity is vital as well, but please don't confuse it with obsequiousness. Glad-handing and flattery might sell a few books, but that's not where the money is. The money is in selling to the same customers over and over. People aren't stupid, especially not the ones who buy books, and they'll see through that kind of Uriah Heepery in a heartbeat. Used car salesmen, junk mail, telemarketers and Internet spam have polarized the buying public against Being Sold To, and in order to make them happy, you have to do a lot more than simply provide them with what they want. You have to engage your customer, make eye contact, make them laugh, discuss the book they're considering intelligently (even if it's only to say "I haven't read it, but people whose opinion I trust like it"), and, in short, treat them as human beings and not as carnie marks. If you can send a new customer away from your table with a smile on his or her face, you're ahead of 60% or more of your competition.

31

Be willing to go the extra few feet in order to stand out from the other dealers competing for that self-same wallet. Have business cards made with your e-mail address (one of them, anyhow) and pass them out. Make bookmarks with the same information, decorated with appropriate clip art, and use them for bag stuffers.

If you don't have the book they want, have them give you *their* email address, and look for that book the next time you go hunting. If you turn it up, contact them immediately. In fact, if you don't have what your customer is looking for, and there's more than one bookseller in the room, make a point of sending your customer to them to see if they have it. The first—and arguably most important—lesson I learned in retail is that the customer gets what they want, whether or not they get it from you. When I was running a used record store, many's the time I would spend 10-15 minutes on the phone calling other shops in the area trying to find some old 45 for a customer who was standing in front of me. More often than not I'd track one down, and he'd be off to spend his money somewhere else. *But*—and it's a big but indeed—he would invariably come back to me, because I invested the time and effort in getting him what he wanted.

And that's the name of the game—bring 'em back alive, and happy.

7

Obtaining Stock

There are, by and large, two ways to obtain books to sell: buying them and trading for them (there's a third way, but it's not reliable enough to make a huge difference. We'll get to it a little later).

The assiduousness with which you hunt is mitigated only by how much you're willing to put yourself out, and/or how enthusiastic you are about spending time and energy plowing through dusty shops, driving to parts of town (or even to other cities) you've never been to before, and bargaining with people for a better price.

When you buy, you have to be extremely careful about price. It doesn't matter how many books you buy or how nice they are if you can't make a profit on them. Know your markets and what they'll bear before laying out the long green, or your hobby will turn into something you'll never be able to justify to your spouse or SO.

Work your local bookshops often enough that they know you by sight—and, not incidentally, are happy to see you come through the door. Get to know the clerks as well as the owners by name, and be ready to pass a little conversation with them if they aren't terribly busy. Make sure that they know you're buying for resale; not only do many booksellers automatically discount to the trade (have a tax number ready), but as long as you're not in direct competition with them, they may be willing to give you other breaks as well.

When out of town, call first to make sure that the owner or manager will be in when you plan to go by. Let them know who you are

33

and why you're coming, and make sure that they have more than a single shelf of whatever it is you're looking for. There's no good reason to trek all the way across a strange town from a hotel room just to look at four ratty copies of *Jurassic Park* or a shelf of movie tie-ins.

When you get to the bookshop, introduce yourself, mentioning you've already called, hand them a card, and ask where they keep what you're interested in. Then be prepared for disappointment.

As a rule, I know in the first five minutes if I'm going to be in any given shop after the sixth; it doesn't take long at all to scope out a bad selection. Don't walk away, though, without scoping it *all* out—you don't know what might be a foot further down the shelf if you don't at least glance that far. But be willing to cut your losses and move on to the next shop, if there is one.

Often enough to make it worthwhile, you won't be disappointed. Oh, you're not going to find a stack of Gnomes and Arkhams in fine condition these days, at least not at a price you can make a profit on (unless you're very, very fortunate indeed), but if you're looking for books to sell to readers, any bookshop with a decent selection will give you plenty of table fodder.

If you're happy with what you're seeing, make a point of asking about buying in quantity. Something along the lines of, "How many would I have to pile up before I can get 20%?" will almost never be taken amiss, since it gives them the option of setting the parameters for the bargain. They want to move stock, and if they can eat 20% or more to move a boxful of books out the door, they'll more than likely be delighted to do it.

They may already have a discount structure in place. One shop I frequently dealt with made it easy: 10 books, 10%; 20 books, 20%, and so on until you got to 50 and above, which got you a whopping 50% discount off the marked price. Since their prices rarely rose above $3, I'd regularly buy several hundred books each time I went there, which pleased them no end; they were paying 25¢ a pop, if that, so almost anything they got above that was gravy. I'll buy $1-3 books at half-price all day, especially since I pick the ones I can sell for $2-5. Turn a nickel into a couple of quarters, and you're doing just fine.

Now, I will warn you that some bookshops will NOT discount to the trade at all. Why, I don't know, but it's their choice and you certainly won't do yourself any good by arguing with them. Not everybody who sells books is a bookman, I suppose. Some people would be just as happy to sell cheap running-shoe knockoffs or that catalog crap you see advertised on TV at three in the morning. These days, with the advent of eBay and ABE, everybody thinks they can sell books, and the long line of tradition and ethics becomes more and more diluted.

If you happen to find a bookseller who's reluctant to cut you a deal, even on a bulk purchase, you have to decide whether or not the possibility of finding something worth your time and effort is worth paying top whack for. I know of a shop in another city where I've rarely been able to wangle a discount, but the prices are so cheap on what I want (and the owner's knowledge of his stock and its value so negligible) that I go back each time I'm in town and still make a profit. Your mileage may vary considerably; learning the difference is part of knowing your craft.

Bookshops aren't the only places from which to buy in bulk, though. I've had an enormous amount of good luck buying in fairly large lots (anywhere from a dozen to 200 books) from eBay sellers.

You have to look carefully at what they're offering, of course, and the condition they say it's in, but it's entirely possible to buy 150 books for less than 75¢ apiece, even with shipping, set aside 60 or so for resale, and then use the rest to trade for something you need more. Unless the books are really, really trashed, it's hard to lose on a deal like that. In many cases, I was the only one bidding on the lot. This is one of the primary ways I restock after a convention. As is true with all eBay transactions, of course, you take chances. Ask the seller as many questions as you need to *before you bid*, and keep his replies. This can come in handy later if you have any disputes about condition, edition, etc.

Keeping an eye on eBay is a good idea for the Good Stuff, too, I'll point out. As I write this, I've recently bought a number of pe-rennial sellers (all SF Book Club titles, see that chapter for details) for 99¢ and postage; again, for whatever reason, I was the only bidder, and I got them for my opening bids. Down the line I know I can sell them without difficulty for at least ten times what I paid—more than that if I want to wait.

Having broached the subject, let's talk about the expensive books. I haven't addressed them much so far, because they're very much a rarified area, especially for a beginning avocational bookseller, but they're an intrinsic part of the business and can't be ignored.

By virtue of their scarcity, they're going to be hard for you to find at all, much less at a price low enough for you to make a profit on. On top of that, they're going to require you to learn a significant amount of essential information, if only to prevent yourself from being fooled or flat-out ripped off. You cannot hope to compete in this arena without a good, solid working knowledge of the small presses, both early and current, and the books and authors they published. This can take an active form, where you spend years reading over catalogs and listings and talking to specialist booksellers; or it can take a passive form, where you spend a lot of money amassing the proper references.

Either way, you have to decide if the learning curve is one you want to tackle, and if so, to what degree. There really is no easy way around this except to shrug it off and concentrate on other areas.

If you want to go this route, then you'll have to take a more proactive tack: you're going to have to advertise for them, and be willing—and able—to buy at competitive prices. You won't find a lot of old fan-press firsts turning up at your local two-for-one shop, it just doesn't happen very much any more. Taking local ads might not be terribly productive, either, unless you live in a fairly large town or city, in which case your competition is going to be greater.

You can take one of those "Best prices for your collection" ads in the prozines, but chances are more than even that you aren't going to be paying the best prices, and let's face it; people with collections to sell rarely answer those ads. They contact the dealer(s) from whom they bought the books in the first place, and sell them back.

Now, there's always the chance that at a con somewhere you might make the acquaintance of an older fan (or the widow or widower of an older fan), get to know him or her, and strike up a relationship that culminates in your being offered their complete set of Fantasy Press firsts in jackets for what is essentially the cost of a month's groceries, but if you hold your breath for this to happen you won't make it to the end of this chapter, let alone the book.

Find every book sale you can, everywhere within a two-hour drive of where you live. Library sales, estate sales, auctions, multi-family yard sales, church and school rummage sales, and so on. Get on as many mailing lists for such things as you can. Hit them all, but do it as systematically as you can, saving as much on gas, wear and tear, and time as is possible. Believe me, you'll have a ball (assuming, as we are, that you love books and book people), and in many cases, one sale's haul will pay for all.

And, to be perfectly honest, there have been people I've met at conventions with whom I struck up conversations that ended with an invitation to make an offer on their books. It does, in fact, happen. But you will *not* catch me holding my breath for it.

There are also times when someone will approach your table at a con, idly look over your stock, then even more idly ask, just in passing, if there might be someone around who might be interested in buying some old science fiction books. You might think about it, then shrug and allow as how you might be interested in looking a few things over, in between customers, you understand. And they may very well think about this, nod and mosey away, tossing back over their shoulder that they might, in fact, bring a few things by for you to look at later on, just in case.

So you wipe the sweat off your palms, hoping and praying that they won't bother to stop at any of the other booksellers' tables, and begin figuring out how much cash you have on hand, how much operating capital you can spare, and checking the balance in your checking account. Just in case.

Then, an hour or so later (or about how long it takes them to go back to their room—or their house, if they're local) they might saunter back in with an old cardboard box and plunk it down in front of you and mention, as they look around the room at the four other booksellers, that you might or might not be interested in what they have, but if not, well...

So you sigh *just* loudly enough to be heard, put a slightly pained, I've-seen-it-all expression on your face, open the box and peer over the tops of your glasses at what they brought you. *If you're smart—* and you'd better be—you'll keep that slightly pained expression on your face no matter what you find in that box. Trust me; they know what they have, you know that they know. It's all part of the dance, and it's a dance you'll have to learn to love. I was born loving it, but that's just me.

After you've gone through the box, looking daggers at those customers who've been watching the whole thing and barely holding in their gasps as each book comes out of it, you make a show of brushing dust and flakes of paper off your shirt, clear your throat (if you can arrange to sneeze a couple of times, it really can help things) and comment that there might be a couple of things in the box you could be interested in if the price was right (brush-brush *sneeze!*), and that for a little more you'd be willing to take the rest off their hands as well (brush *sneeze!*).

They might nod and frown as if thinking it over, then allow as how it really might be too much trouble to lug that heavy box around to the other dealers in the room (who by now have sniffed the air, heard the peculiar music this dance requires and are barely holding their individual bottles) and then ask you how much you might be willing to pay?

At this point, the dance ceases to be a relaxed, composed fox-trot and becomes a toe-to-toe, cheek-to-cheek lambada, and you'd better be ready for it. Offer too little right away and all of a sudden that box will be light enough for them to carry across the room to the next guy; offer too much, and you'll diddle yourself out of some profit.

You make an offer, somewhere comfortably under what you expect to pay, but not so much so that your partner in this terpsichorean exercise takes offense. He peers at you through slitted lids, shakes his head, and says he was hoping for a bit more than that.

You can still lose at this point, so be careful with your next offer. It should be, of course, higher than the first one, but still under whatever maximum amount you have in mind (you do have one in mind, right? Well, then, go back and come up with one).

The dance continues, with one degree of civility or another, until you both decide on a price that makes you happy—or you don't, and he walks over to bookseller #2, who probably has deeper pockets than you.

If you do come to an understanding, pay up happily, get a receipt for tax purposes, and (this is vitally important, but is one of those things you might not think of on your own) *refrain from pricing and selling the books until he is out of the room.* This just makes sense. You don't want to slap him in the face with how much profit you're going to make from his willingness to sell at a lower price than you were willing to pay, even though he knows you're going to. It's impolite. Let him walk away and sit in the hotel bar and tell stories about the dealer he got top dollar from for a bunch of old books.

Once he's gone home, or to a panel, you can take over his stool and tell *your* side of it. (I will point out that the above scenario did, in fact, happen to me a few years ago. It was a box of pulps, and the first one I pulled out was a Clayton *Astounding*. I got them much cheaper than I expected, priced them as quickly as I could, and sold them all but the few I kept for myself before the room closed that evening. Sometimes the magic works…).

At some point, you're going to buy in bulk, either online or in person, and in all likelihood more than once. This means you're going to accumulate books that are of no real use to you as a seller, for whatever reasons: they aren't nice enough, or they're off-genre, or they're too new/too old, or just not what you like to sell. Fair enough, but what do you do with them?

That brings us to the second primary method of acquiring stock, trading for it. This is by far the most wallet-friendly, but it has its limitations, too. First of all, you have to have something to trade that the other guy wants. It doesn't have to be books, of course, but that's probably what you have the most of on hand. Nevertheless, if your partner in this exchange doesn't want tie-in novels and all you have is old *X-Files* and *Stargate: Atlantis* paperbacks, you're boned.

There are almost always one or two locally owned two-for-one bookshops in your area, probably more than that. They love to have new stock and many of them are concerned more with condition than subject. If what you have is old (or as the eBay yobbos have it, "vintage") and in nice shape but something other than you can sell, they'll certainly welcome it; if what you have is ratty, falling apart or crumbling (brush-brush *sneeze*), and you don't want to read them yourself, toss them in the recycling bin and save a tree or two.

Trading has more than one benefit. First and foremost, all you're really out of pocket on is gas money. Second, what you have there in one location is a selection of books you'd otherwise have to drive ALL OVER the place to get to.

So what do you do? You box them up and take them to one or more of those local shops and trade them in for something you *can* sell, is what you do. Figure this out, now: you've got 200 books, none of which are of any value to you except as insulation or door-stops. You load them in the back of your car, drive to the used-paperback shop, and lug them in. They will then give you credit for up to 100 books you *can* sell, and your cost above and beyond what you paid for the books is negligible. I have books in inventory right now that I got in trade for books I got in trade for books I got in trade, and by this time whatever cash I laid out originally for the books I turned around and traded in is buried so deep you couldn't find it with a backhoe. Trade often enough and you're left with a profit margin that will make it a lot easier to justify costlier stuff down the line.

This requires frequent visits to your favorite bookshops, though, as their stock will most likely change from week to week and you don't want to miss something juicy. Then, too, what you can walk away with is limited to what someone else has brought in, and is still there waiting for you; certain classics, like *The Demolished Man* and

Canticle for Leibowitz disappear pretty quickly, as do more current favorites like Terry Pratchett and Kim Stanley Robinson. Still, you don't have to use your credit up all at once, and if you put the titles you look for most often on a list, they'll probably be willing to hold them for you next time they come in.

It's possible to trade in other ways, too, of course. I have no problem with someone bringing me a bag or box of books while I'm at a con, as long as they understand that I may not be able to look them over right away. I cherry-pick in these cases more often than not, if only because I don't want to lug home another 50-60 books on top of leftover stock. I name a price equal to what I think the books are worth at my retail, and we either dicker a little, or they accept, or they move on.

The third way—and it does happen, but not often enough for it to be a major and reliable factor—is when friends present you with a bagful of their leftovers and rejects, particularly when they're faced with moving them. Usually, they're not interested in trade (of course not, they're trying to get rid of books), and here again, what you can't use yourself goes in the trade-in box. (Recently, a friend gave me a huge crate of left-over books, including a complete set of Jim Baen's paperback magazine, *Destinies*. They went right on my own shelf, not the trade box.

8

Managing Your Stock

Inventory

If you're at all serious about doing this right, you're going to need to think about keeping track of your inventory. You have to know what you have, if only so that you don't end up with unnecessary duplicates. It's not hard to do, once you get it started, and it more or less maintains itself without too much work on your part.

Now, you could get fancy with a spread-sheet (like Excel) or database and descriptions, which is fine, but for my purposes (cheap paperbacks, remember) I don't need a lot of who-shot-John. On the other hand, the books I list online are fully described; the difference is that the inventory I keep for my con stock is for my use only, not for publication. It's just the way I keep track of what I have and the price, not an aid to making a sale.

The whole thing is very process-oriented, as is a lot of what I do as a bookseller. I'll describe the process, and you are free to adopt or adapt it to your own circumstances: Books come in. I price them, and then list them (author, title and price) in the master inventory file. In the case of duplicates, highest price goes first, and when I pack the boxes for a convention, that's the way they go in. This inventory list is printed out, and I take it with me as a reference. After a convention, I mark the books I've sold off the list, and then delete them from the master inventory file. This gives me a running inventory, and I can tell at a glance what I still have, and by comparing the corrected list to the master file, what I need to replace. There's a little more to the process, but that's the bulk of it.

In the case of hardcovers, or any book auctioned online, the process is different. You'll want a spread-sheet or database, ideally one specifically set up for keeping a book inventory.

Storage

This is an important point. Poor storage can destroy your stock, so where and how you pack it away should be carefully considered. If your house is anything like ours, there's not a snowball's chance that you have adequate bookshelf space for your own collection, much less sale stock. There are ways around this. If you have an extra closet, install a set of shelves. This can give you 30-50' of space for books that would otherwise end up stacked teeteringly on the floor, or stuffed into boxes stacked teeteringly on the floor.

If you have to store books in boxes, make sure it's short term (under a couple of years ideally) unless you want to go to the expense of acid-free storage boxes, which can add significantly to your CoDB. Place the books in the boxes flat, with the spines turned in. Print out a list of what's in each box, and tape it to the outside of the box. If you sell something out of a box, be sure to mark it off the list.

If you intend to store books for longer than that, then you need to look into archival materials; any good library supply company can sell you the necessary. But don't store them that long, really. Books are organic and need to breathe, and I'm not being new-ageist here. Paper and cloth need air to prevent certain molds, and they need to be isolated from temperature and humidity extremes.

If you're going to keep them for longer than a couple of years, take 'em out of the boxes and put 'em on shelves in your den, preferably out of direct sunlight.

Repair

In a word, don't. You aren't trained for it, and you'll most likely make it worse than it already was. The single exception I make is to re-glue cheap paperbacks into loose covers, and even this is tricky. I knew a guy who could cure cocked spines on paperbacks with a microwave, but every time I've tried it I've screwed it up. Sell the books as-is, without trying to fix them or hide the faults. Unless you're experienced at this, and few of us are, just leave well enough alone.

The Care and Feeding of Books

Whether you're planning to sell them or keep them for your own collection (you greedy fink, you), books need to be protected, and not just from the five elements: sun, water, temperature, kids with sticky fingers and pets with unreliable sphincters. Paperbacks, hardbacks, pulps or digests, you need to keep them clean. This isn't difficult, but you'll have to lay out a bit of capital, and possibly do some hand-work.

Plastics. Not a quote from *The Graduate*, but something you're going to need, both for your Avons and your Arkhams. Not just any plastic, though, but something archival. Mylar D, if you can get it, especially for hardbacks, but certainly polyester and *not* polyethylene; the latter can accelerate the oxidation of paper and that's precisely what you don't want. Oxidation makes cheap paper turn brown and brittle, and whereas polyester is inert, polyethylene ain't; it tends to outgas and speeds up paper's deterioration. For hardbacks, you'll want to cover the dust jackets securely (just like libraries do), and for paperbacks, you'll want to invest in bags.

Why? Simple; one of the most common types of damage books suffer is rubbing, the action of one book scuffing against another as you take it down from the shelf and put it back. Since a significant percentage of the value of a book is the condition of the cover, this is something you should be prepared to prevent.

Dependable and durable book ends.

Let's address paperbacks first. As a rule, I don't like to seal a book up, since trapping air in a bag that holds a book is not a terribly good idea. Almost all paperback bags are designed with a top flap that can be folded (and/or taped) down, which is fine for protecting the tops of the pages clean and dust-free but not so good if you want to keep the rate of oxidation down.

I do tape down the flaps, mostly to prevent dusting but also because it's so much neater (when you have several thousand paperbacks that really is a concern), so what I do to prevent gasses from building up in the bags is to clip the two lower corners. This doesn't expose much, if any, of the book's covers, and it keeps bad air out of the bag. So, since our purpose here is to prevent both rubbing and oxidation, Bob's your uncle.

You can find bags for paperbacks, pulps, digests and just about anything else all over the Internet, but I prefer Bags Unlimited (http://www.bagsunlimited.com/) because I like their pricing and selection. They offer numerous sizes, from thin nurse-novel to beach brick, and you can buy in bulk. (You might also be able to buy these through local comic shops, as they service that field as well.) Shop around, though, and find the best price and quality for your purposes. Just don't cheap out—believe me, the polyester bags are worth it. They don't get cloudy, they look great, and you don't have to replace them every couple of years.

For most hardcovers, focus on the jackets, as that's where a considerable percentage of the value is. In many cases, a fine jacket can represent as much as 75% of the overall value of the book; after all, they get ripped, price-cut, chipped, soiled, creased, stained, frayed, sunned, worn or just tossed away, which prevents them from doing their job protecting the books themselves from suffering any and/or all of the above.

Jacket protectors come in different heights and thicknesses, from 1 to 2 mil. My particular preference is for 1.5, as it's less expensive and, for my purposes, more than adequate. Libraries tend to go for the 2 mil, but they have to contend with multiple check-outs, books going on and of shelves all the time, and readers who have kids with sticky fingers and pets with unreliable sphincters. You're going to treat your stock better than that, not to mention your own collection, right?

I've found that the 12 inch height will accommodate 90% of the books I own and sell, with a little trimming or

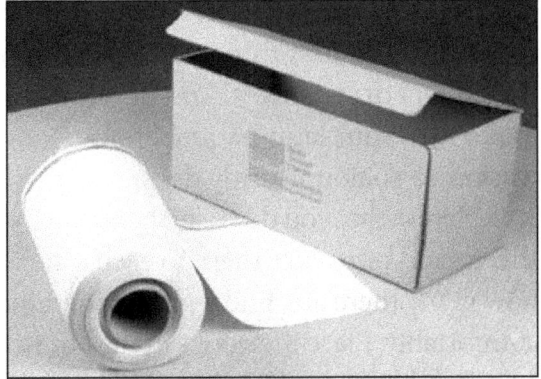

Book protectors come in rolls for easy sizing and dispensing.

folding. Almost every source for these jacket protectors offers a price break for three 300' rolls, but that's a *lot* of jacket protection, even if you're doing this full-time. Protectors also come pre-cut, but I really do prefer the rolls if only because it means less waste. At this writing, prices for the 12 inch, 300 foot rolls run between $48 and $55 plus shipping, but this is one of the few things you shouldn't stinge out on. There's a slim possibility that you can find an office supply store that either carries them or will allow you to order through them and thus avoid shipping charges, but hold not thy breath.

Check online for the various library supply outfits. I use Vernon, but your mileage may very well vary. If you do go to Vernon, look for their "Easy Fit" covers; they open at the bottom rather than in the center, and are a lot easier to use.

Aside from the obvious benefit of keeping the jacket from collecting rips and stains, there is the added advantage of making your books look really *nice* either on your own shelves or at your table. It's a significant selling point whether you're offering it on eBay or in a convention hucksters' room.[6]

If you buy lots off of eBay or at an auction, you're eventually going to have to cope with smelly books. It's inevitable, really. People smoke, and smoke odors only get worse, not better. When books have been in storage for years, they get musty if not moldy, and all that can add up to a snoot-full of *ick*.

There's a way to do away with this, though, and it's actually pretty simple. The first thing you'll need is a box of cheap (the cheaper the better) dryer sheets. You know, the ones you toss in the dryer to make sure your laundry smells sweet, not the ones you throw in the washer to soak up runny dyes.

Here's what you do. Take those smelly books and those cheap dryer sheets, and introduce them to each other. No, seriously. Depending on how many there are, find a plastic container large enough to hold them comfortably. Place the books in the bin with a dryer sheet between each one. Put the lid on the box and leave them for a couple of days. I guarantee that at the end of that time, they'll be odor-free (well, they'll smell like dryer sheets for a day or so, but that will pass). Single books can be treated by sticking them with a dryer sheet, in a Ziploc bag.

Why cheap sheets? Because they won't leave gunk on your books, that's why. And they really, really work! Isn't that amazing? They really do, in all seriousness. I once bought a signed copy of Donald Wollheim's first hardback anthology, the smallish (if rich) *Portable Novels of Science* (Viking 1945). Even before I opened the package I could smell the stale smoke, and when I got the book out, it damn near knocked me over. It positively *reeked*. I had to put dryer sheets every ten pages, not to mention wrapping them around the book itself, but it's as fresh as the driven daisies now.

Mold can be treated fairly easily, too, by putting the affected book in a plastic bag and stashing it in your freezer for a few days. It will kill the mold, but marks may still remain. Please do *not* do what I once heard a typical yobbo suggest and rub your book with dilute bleach. *Please*. I don't think that's asking too much.

Pricing

How do you put a price on a book? You have to do it; you can't just give them away (except, of course, to me). What do you use for guidelines?

You'd think the answer would be complicated, and, well, it is. A bit, anyway. It takes knowledge of what comparable books have sold for, and whether or not that price is aberrant. It takes knowledge of what your customer base will bear in terms of cost-for-quality. It takes knowledge of the relative rarity (or non-rarity) of the book in question, and it depends entirely on condition and what you laid out for it in the first place.

Researching a book is really pretty easy, what with this new Internet thing. You check AddAll.com, you check closed eBay auctions. You note the condition of your book, and try to match it with one or more of those listed on those sites. If you see 30 copies, and five of them match yours in terms of condition, look at the price spread. If it runs $20–25, you can probably assume yours will sell at a comparable price. Ignore, though, the highest prices, since in most cases they won't sell until the others do. When in doubt, price towards the low end; you want to sell the book, not put it on display. *Nobody* gets rich selling used books.

The paperbacks I sell at conventions are priced from $1 to $6, with a very few exceptions selling for more. My price is predicated mostly on condition, although an earlier printing of a specific title will be priced higher than a later one if both are in nice shape. And I routinely discount for anyone who buys more than one book at one time, usually 10–15%, rounded up to the next whole dollar. The cold reality is that most paperbacks just aren't worth more than a few dollars unless they're originals by popular authors in very nice condition.

There's no hard and fast rule here, except that I know what I've sold them for in the past, and I figure if I'm a bit high on a particular book, encouraging the browser to buy by the handful will take care of any inequity. There have been any number of times when a buyer has stopped by my tables, grabbed everything by Heinlein (or Doc Smith or Sturgeon or Simak) after I've given them my patented "The more you buy, the better the deal" spiel.

With rare books, your research needs to be a little deeper. Find out as much as you can about the book in whatever references you have access to. Sure, you want to sell your stock rather than hang on to it, but there's no point in selling a $100 Gnome Press book in fine condition for $20, even if it only cost you 25¢. Make sure your research is correct. Don't be afraid to ask questions. Call a local bookseller who specializes in rare or antiquarian books, but keep your questions short and to the point, and do not, under any circumstances, misrepresent yourself. Just tell them you're a bear of little brain, and most of them will be happy to help educate you.

The three basic factors for deciding on price are: condition, scarcity, and demand. This is the three-legged stool all booksellers sit on to do business. If a book is dirt-common, it doesn't matter if it's in as-new condition. On the other hand, if it's rare enough, condition means less and less. Twenty years ago, ex-library copies were anathema to booksellers, either being returned to the library from which they'd been stolen or dumped in the quarter-bins outside on the sidewalk with the Readers' Digest Condensed Books and old issues of National Geographic. These days, an otherwise clean ex-lib copy of a rare book can go for $100 or more. Go figure.

Condition is perhaps the hardest to nail down, since it's something that research can do little to define. The ABAA site at http://abaa.org/ has a primer for new booksellers that explains terminology. Knowing a chip from a closed tear from a bumped corner is something every seller of even moderately rare books is expected to know, so spend some time with it. Believe me; it will pay off, if only so that knowledgeable buyers will be able to trust you. That's a valuable commodity these days.

Scarcity and demand are tied together. If there are 100,000 copies of a book available, but 110,000 people want it, the price is going to be higher than if only 50,000 did. Considering that many of the small-press books from the Golden Age (for my purposes, from 1939 – the year Arkham House was created – to 1960) had print runs of fewer than 5,000, it's no wonder that collectors pay gazillions for books that are readily available as reprints.

Demand isn't just based on rarity, though. Popular authors, or books considered to be "classics," will have higher prices than less desirable titles with lower print runs from the same publisher because there are more people searching for them just to read, not collect. However the archivist in me might quail because *Sixth Column* by Heinlein will always sell for more money than *The Philosophical Corps* by Edward B. Cole in spite of the fact that the latter book is scarcer, that's the way the market works.

Here's why: comic and paperback collectors have popularized the term "key book," which, however contrived, is at least reasonably apt. Van Vogt's *Slan* is a "key book;" Max Ehrlich's *The Big Eye*, while it may have been the very first Doubleday sf title, ain't a "key" unless you're collecting all the Doubleday sf books. And good luck if you are. A collector who wants to assemble a good basic library of fantastic literature with a limited budget needs to concentrate his or her efforts on the Major League hitters, not the Minors.[7]

One of the major mistakes booksellers can make – especially those tied to brick & mortar shops – is pricing books at what they might be worth in a large metropolitan area rather than where they actually are. If you've got a little shop in Frog Level, Virginia, you simply cannot expect your walk-in trade to be willing to spend New York money. A book that's easily worth $100 in Manhattan may only bring $20 in Frog Level, if that much, and if you think you'll eventually sell that book for its NYC price, you might as well open a museum.

You'd think that the Internet would even this out, making that book worth as much one place as another, but when you factor in the other 999 booksellers with the same title at a similar price, any field-leveling goes by the board. Price your books according to what your local traffic will bear—that way, even if you find yourself in a WorldCon huckster room, your stock will fly out the door instead of walking. If you've been careful about buying, you're going to make a profit anyway, so why not be the least expensive bookseller in the room?[8]

Online sales aren't always necessarily indicative of real-world values, either, especially auctions. There are expenses involved with listing online that can make a significant difference in your profit margin. Say you have a book priced at $40. You should already have most of your expenses figured into that price, whatever they might be. List that book online, and you add whatever it costs you to log on in the first place, plus the cost of whichever listing service you're using, plus any cut they might take if the book sells.

This is going to add up to at least a few dollars. You can mitigate this by listing a big load of books, thereby spreading the costs thinner, but now we're adding in the cost in time and effort (and money, if you hire someone to do it) of listing all those extra titles with descriptions and prices. Not to mention the other 200 copies listed by other sellers. Now all of a sudden that book that would have sold quite nicely at $40 at a con (or, if you have a shop, out the door) is struggling to sell at all, with a slimmer margin than you began with.

This is, of course, a caveat and not a blanket dismissal of online selling. There are plenty of booksellers for whom selling online is a life-saver. Just be aware of the costs here, as you are with conventions.

Auctions can be your best return, but the flip side is that they can be your worst, too. There are a number of online auctions, but as of this writing eBay is still the king, so we'll use them as a guide.

There are so many factors involved with listing a book on eBay that it comes close to boggling the mind. What color should the background be? What color should the text be? How many pictures, and how big? Should I use my logo? Should I link to my home page? How many secondary categories should I list, if any? Is it a good idea to set a reserve? What should the opening bid be? What about the "buy it now" option? And on and on, *ad infinitum et ad nauseum*.

I'm not even going to try to address most of those questions, since this isn't principally a book about buying and selling on eBay. I will tell you, though, that simple is best. Anything that causes your listing to take an inordinate time to load will cost you potential bidders. Huge photos, moving banners, music (why on earth *anyone* would want to slow down the bidding process by adding a WAV file—or worse, an MP3—to their listing is beyond me), complicated graphics… If the screen takes more than a few seconds to load, chances are you've lost a potential sale.

I will admit that it has become easier to jazz up your listing on eBay in the past few years, of course. Links, fonts, logos; they're more common all the time, and with most bidders using high-speed access these days if you stay away from the damned music and videos, you'll be okay. All I ask is that you don't put the photos of the book three or four scrolls down. Please?

You absolutely have to have photos or scans of your items, I believe that utterly. But you don't have to have more than 3-4 in most cases, and if you're smart about using the PhotoMerge feature in PhotoShop (or its equivalent), you can combine two or more photos into one larger one.

I use a scanner instead of a digital camera, simply because it's easier and because books are flat. But there's nothing inherently better or more advantageous about one over the other, so pick whichever works best for you.

By and large, I scan only the front cover; this is sufficient in most cases. However, if there's damage to the rear or spine panel, or if the book has edition points visible only on the rear cover, I'll do the whole thing, even if it's too big to scan in one pass. Again, PhotoMerge or any of the variations thereon are a big help. Rule of thumb should be that if there's a flaw in the jacket or book big enough to be mentioned in the description, scan it so your bidders are completely aware of it. This will serve to show that you can be trusted, and will also give you a better position if a bidder challenges you later.

Another reason to scan more than the front cover is if the book you're offering is one you expect to get more than, say, $50 for. If you want your bidders to open up their wallets, you owe it to them to give them as complete a picture (heh) as you can. If it's signed, then by all means include a picture of the signature/inscription—but do *not* scan it if it's on an interior page; use a camera. Need I explain why? Stressing the binding, however briefly, is an invitation to the Demon of Broken Hinges, the worst kind of bibliophilic hubris.

Here's something I've been running into more and more recently, something that I feel strongly about (like you've been *sooo* calm up to now, Webster). I've been seeing more and more items listed on eBay not with actual photos of the copy being offered, but with a stock photo of a brand-new copy, no matter what the condition of the item itself. Apparently, either eBay flips a coin when deciding whether or not to label the photo as stock, or the seller can delete that label, because only about one in five that I've seen actually say it's stock.

Do I really have to explain this one? It's simple. Unless you are selling a brand new copy, unread, with absolutely no flaws, *completely untouched by hand of man*, using a stock photo can be seen as misleading at best, and dishonest at worst. It's all part of making yourself as trustworthy to your bidders as possible.

The best advice I can give you is Keep It Simple. Don't worry about fancy colors, or fonts, or music, or animated graphics, or any of the other trappings some eBay sellers are convinced make them stand out from the rest. If you have a logo, by all means use it, but don't go crazy. Use a big enough typeface to be easily readable, make sure your photos are color-corrected and big enough to see clearly, make sure your description of the book is accurate, be sure to insert any general instructions or information into each listing, and you're pretty much covered. Anything else is icing (and can be pretty expensive icing, too—those seemingly nickel-and-dime charges add up), and should be decided on an item-by-item basis.

Stand out by building a solid reputation for your honesty, integrity, skills at packing and speed of shipping, not how many typefaces you use or the cute dancing hamsters cha-cha-ing around the borders. Believe me, if your customers keep coming back for the books you're selling and because they know your rep is as a reliable and dependable bookseller, they aren't gonna give the hind end of a rat how many colors you've used in the text.

And please, I beg of you: if you use a camera instead of a scanner, make sure that the photo(s) you use for the listing are *in focus*. That's right; not blurry or smeared or wobbly or anything other than crystal clear. If you're offering one book or fifty, make sure that your bidders can see what they're bidding on well enough to feel confidant about plunking down their hard-earned coinage.

Like a lot of people, I check eBay every day, and if I see a listing without a photo I don't even bother to click on it. If the photos used in the listing are blurred, chances are almost 100% that I won't bid. What's more, if they look like they've been taken from the top of the stairs, what's the point of using them at all? In focus, please, and close enough that your bidders can read the front cover (or whichever angle you're doing). Backgrounds should be neutral, titles should be clearly legible, and don't stint on the number of photos just because eBay charges more to add them. Post the front and any flaws, and then add a line to your listing telling your bidders that you have more images available and all they have to do is request them. When they do (and they will, if they're serious), send them as soon as you get their note; you've only got a week or so for your basic auction, give them plenty of time to make up their minds.

If you have multiple listings, you might want to consider using specialized online auction software. It can make a real difference in how long it takes to upload, say, 30 books or more. You can take your time putting descriptions and photos together, making decisions about ancillary eBay options, then once you're done, run them all up the line at once. I've found that this is a really big help. Not only do all your auctions start at once, they end within a few minutes, and you can take care of billing and emails in an hour or so, depending on how many items you list at a time.

So, when should you start your auction? Good question. A friend of mine swears by 8pm Sunday night, which, assuming you've opted for the standard 7-day auction, ends exactly a week later. This, he opines, gives everybody a chance to get home from a weekend's debauchery, unpack the car, and settle in to check their e-mail.

To be honest, I haven't found that 8pm Sunday is much different from, say, 7pm Thursday, but the idea of not-too-early, not-too-late is sound. You want to catch people before they go to bed, but after dinner. And don't forget what I said back in chapter five about seasonal differences.

While we're discussing eBay, please allow me to mention a few things that may very well hold you back. Here's the first: when describing a book, try very hard not to use the unfortunate phrase "In good condition for its age." I see this all the time, and it's an immediate tip-off that I'm looking at total cluelessness. This insidious little idiom looks, at first glance, perfectly useful. It isn't. It is utterly meaningless, devoid of any real context, and serves no purpose other than to prove to the book people looking at your listing that you don't know what you're talking about.

Condition is an absolute. A brand new book in fine condition is the same as a one-hundred year-old book in fine condition. Your purpose in describing the book must be accuracy, not approximation. It's either in "good condition," full stop, or it isn't.

Be objective when describing a book you want to sell. "Well, if this were a new book, it would be pretty sucky, but since it's thirty years old (or twenty or ten), it's actually pretty good!" You really want that on your antiquarian-bookseller's conscience? There are still books out there, even paperbacks, which could still pass for new. I own a number of them myself.

As long as I'm foaming at the mouth about nomenclature, allow me to raise another point, if I may. If you're trying to sell, say, the May 1950 issue of *Astounding*, or the first issue of *Galaxy*, or a random issue of *F&SF* from the '70s, do try hard not to describe it as a "pulp," okay? Those aforementioned periodicals are, in fact, digests. The fiction contained therein may be pulpish, but the magazines themselves aren't, by definition.

The term "pulp" refers to a specific magazine format, seven by ten inches, although there are minor variations in those dimensions. The larger nine by twelve format, as used by the original *Amazing Stories* (among others), as well as by *Analog* for a couple of dozen issues from 1963 to 1965, are called "bedsheets." Pulps aren't digests; digests aren't bedsheets; and vice-versa. Yeah, you can talk about your magazine collection without having to add that some are digests and others are something else, but when you're offering them for sale you need to be specific.

I know it seems to be overly-persnickety hair-splitting, but collectors tend to take this sort of thing quite seriously. If you use the right terminology, whether in describing old magazines or leather-bound incunabula, your customers will feel a lot more secure about your own levels of knowledge.

When you post an item for auction, make your opening price reasonable. I don't mean cheap, of course, but if you expect to get $100 for a book starting the auction at $95 will keep more potential buyers from bidding than anything else. Keep it reasonable and the bids will pile up; auctions aren't about the final price as much as they are about the number of bids. The more bids and bidders there are and the more competition there is among your customers, the better that final price is likely to be.

"Reasonable" also means "sensible." Does it make any sense to start a book at $600 when there are five other copies running at the same time that start at $35? As René Descartes said just before he disappeared, I think not. Buyers search eBay for what they want by keywords, which will show them almost everything being offered by a specific author or publisher (or whatever else you're using as a keyword), and you can bet that their competition is doing the same thing. This means that when they find those five other copies at $35, your $600 offering will gather dust and cobwebs.

Do some searching yourself, in fact. If you've got a heavy-hitter book, one you expect to get three figures for, spend a week or so keeping track of what other copies of the same book are selling for in other auctions. Find all the copies currently being sold and add them to your "Watch" list. See what the opening bids are, see how they end up, and check out how many bidders there are. Plan your own opening bid accordingly.

Keywords. Let's talk about that for a bit. My daily searches are set up by authors' names—Clifford Simak, Henry Kuttner, etc.—or by titles, such as "A Game of Thrones" or "Science Fiction Hall of Fame;" or by publisher, like Gnome Press or Arkham House. If the seller isn't careful with his/her spelling, those of us who search that way will miss that listing and the seller will miss a sale.

It is incumbent on you the seller, therefore, to make sure that you spell names and words correctly. Spelling *does* count. I can go on for hours about this, of course, with plenty of extra verbiage concerning those damn kids on my lawn and the music they listen to, but this isn't a matter of some old guy bitching about a bunch of noise. This is *business*. It follows, of course, that you spell names and other words right when you search, but that should go without saying.

And please do me one other favor. Ending your opening bid (or buy-it-now price) with something weird is just silly. There's no good reason to set that price at, say, $5.63. I mean, why? What's wrong with $5.50? Or even $5.99? Those odd numbers to the right of the decimal just make bookkeeping a little harder for everybody. I don't mean to be Adrian Monk here, but c'mon.

9

Pros and Cons

"Pros and cons of what?" you ask. Well, that's not quite what I meant. I'm talking about professional writers selling their own books at conventions.

There are a couple of ways to do this. You can, if you're of a mind to, buy a table in the dealers' room and sit behind it eight hours a day. This may hamper your social life just a bit, and keep you from participating in panels and such. Some writers may see this as a reasonable trade-off, but chances are that the convention committee wouldn't agree—after all, they invited you with the idea that you *would* natter on with other guests on various abstruse subjects for the edification of their paying attendees.

Some cons will give you a table, especially if you're a big enough name to do a signing, but that's generally only for an hour or so, at which time it's the next pro's turn. So what can you do?

What I've done in the past, with ample success, is to cut a deal with my fellow pros. I'm going to be behind that table most of the weekend anyhow, except for the few hours I'm on panels myself, and I'm doing the very thing they want to be doing for at least a few hours themselves and may not be able to: selling books.

If you're a pro scheduled to appear as a guest at a convention, contact the committee member who's running the room and ask them for a list of the booksellers who've bought tables. Don't wait too long, but don't ask right away; there are times when the room doesn't fill up until a few weeks before that weekend of the con and

they may not have all the booksellers reg-
istered. For that matter, in these days of
hucksters' rooms selling practically everything *but* books, you may have to make a
deal with somebody hawking jewelry, or
plush dragons, or anime DVDs.

When you have a list of the sellers
you need, contact them and ask if any of
them might be willing to give you some
table space in return for payment, either
in cash or trade. Until we stopped going
to the same conventions, I had a running

Plexiglass easel perfect
for displaying.

agreement with a well-known writer to display copies of his books
at my table. When he did a reading, or a panel, or especially a signing, he would mention that his books were for sale at my table and
fans would flock to me and buy. I kept single copies of each title on
display, cover out on easels, and sold from boxes under the table.
These were brand new copies selling for cover price, hardcover and
paperback.

For this consignment service, I charged him 20%. Since he was
buying copies at 45-50%, this still gave him a profit, and I made
$1.40 a throw on a $6.99 paperback, and $4.60 or so on hardbacks.
Considering the small amount of table-space his books were taking
up, this was a more than reasonable return. Since many of those
buyers came back and bought other books from me, I made out
pretty well and so did he.

The writer was happy for other reasons as well, as he didn't have
to lug those damned heavy books around all weekend. He could
hang out with his fans, go to lunch, listen to the GoH speech, secure
in the knowledge that I was working just as hard to sell his books as
I was my regular stock.

I have an advantage over a lot of other writers in that I have no
trouble finding somebody to sell my books: it's that big hairy guy
under the propeller-fez. This means that I'm already half-disposed
to sell for the other pros at the con. There's a definite benefit to this

that goes beyond just helping out one of the guests, it gives you a cachet that makes you valuable to the whole convention committee as someone who makes and keeps their guests happy.

Equally, if you're going to be a dealer at a con, check the guest roster. Note the names of professionally published writers (the self-publishers are on their own) and contact them through the con-chair or guest liaison. Offer them space at your table if they'd like it, and let them know what your terms are. I charge 20%, but others might go higher—Steve Miller and Sharon Lee, for example, are willing to offer as much as 30%.

Go them one better, in fact, and once they've been confirmed as guests, scout up as many of their titles in the used book stores or online auctions and add them to your inventory, even if it's only for that one con. Give the attendees a choice of both new and out-of-print books by the author(s) they've come to see. Chances are excellent that those guests will be delighted to sign any old books you have, and that reaches beyond the convention weekend to any and all conventions or auctions down the line. The more books by a guest the attendees find, the happier they are, and thus the happier those guests will be as well.

There's another aspect of this that bears mentioning, too. Having five or six people standing around your table handing you money for a guest's new books will almost always attract even more people, curious to see what's going on. Once they see what you're selling, and once you make eye contact and genially ask them what they might be looking for, you can turn that 20% consignment into more and more money. Nickels into whole bunches of quarters, remember? Besides, it certainly can't help to make contact with and do business with the people who create the very objects you love yourself, right?

Very important: keep track of the numbers. It doesn't have to be anything elaborate; I list the titles of each book on a sheet of paper, then make a hash-mark for each one sold under that title. Easy-peezy, brush-and-sneezy. That sheet of paper can be your receipt—ask one of the con volunteers to run it to the hotel office and ask for a Xerox of it, and you each have a copy. Pay the writer *in cash*, unless he or she is willing to take your check or (even better) is willing to take it in trade. Don't hold your breath for that, though, writers get a little faint at the sight of cash.

What, though, if you're a writer who *doesn't* have new stock to sell? This is far more common in my experience than the pro with boxfuls of books they got from the publisher. How does one go about bringing in new stock when there are no new booksellers in the room?

This can be a little more complicated, and you may have to work a deal with the convention. An established convention, one which has been around for a decade or more, usually has what for lack of a better term I'll call a "discretionary fund." This fund can be used to set up an account with a local chain bookstore through which the convention can purchase new titles by their guest(s) at a discount, and then return unsold copies for credit. As those copies will almost certainly be signed by the author(s), said chain store will be getting back more than they gave. Do this three or four years in a row without problems on your end, and the chain store will be delighted to help in other ways such as displays, in-store advertising (if they do, reciprocate by hanging their logo over the signing table) and so on.

The convention can either sell the books themselves in the room or at registration, or contract with one of the sellers in the room to do it for them. For consideration, of course.

If you're a pro, make sure that the convention has actually scheduled a signing for you. I've been to cons all too many times over the years where the program didn't include signings and fans had to catch their idols on the fly. For someone with a couple of paperbacks or a hardcover to get signed this isn't much of a hardship, but what about those of us with a bucketful?

If there isn't a signing for you, make sure you get through the dealers' room at least two of three times throughout the weekend, and sign whatever copies the sellers have. Linger, if you will, so that your fans can catch up to you and get you to sign *their* books. Alternatively, you can set up in the bar and sign. Bars like crowds.

(I'm reminded of a convention a few years ago where I was a guest, and given an hour to sign in the hotel restaurant. I had a nice, quiet lunch. Such is the life of the little-known scrivener.)

If you're willing to travel off-campus, you can always arrange for a signing at a local indy or specialty shop (if there are any) or at one of the chains, but this can cut the convention proper out of the loop, which may not be the best thing for you to do. You're in town, after all, for the con, not Books-A-Million. No reason you can't do both, of course, and chances are if you ask nicely and do your duty to the con-com, they'll even drive you there and back.

Let's address one more point here, if I may. If you are a seller, and you have an ordinary book by a guest and he or she signs it, please don't insult your clientele by doubling the price. If it's a rare book, by all means go for it, but your average reader copy shouldn't get a price hike just because the author signed it. Yes, there is an added value, but that value varies from individual author to individual author (not to mention from reader to reader) and it's very tough to quantify. As a rule, signatures from living authors add minimal *monetary* value to a book, although the intrinsic value can be enormous to someone who doesn't frequent the convention circuit or otherwise hang with famous writers.

If said author is a major player, or someone who doesn't go to conventions very often, all bets are off. There's a joke among booksellers concerning some very accessible and eager authors that their unsigned books are worth more than signed ones; when the latter far outnumber the former, it's a joke we make with one raised eyebrow.

What else can I say on the subject? Pros, treat your cons well; cons, do the same for your guests. Sellers, respect those who've worked hard to create what you're selling and don't try to weasel them; authors, if the seller flogs a couple of dozen copies for you, inscribe one for them just to see them smile.

◆ 10 ◆

Packing & Shipping

Okay, you've sold it and gotten payment for it. What's next? Whether you're selling online or through a catalog, the most important aspect of your business once you've gotten payment is getting the book to your customer in the same condition you sold it to them. I cannot emphasize this enough.

We've almost certainly all received an expensive book in the mail from some bozo who tossed it in an ordinary manila envelope without any attempt to safeguard it from the tender mercies of the USPS or some other delivery service. Invariably, it arrived with the jacket torn or crumpled, the page edges mauled, and/or the boards dinged by other, heavier packages.

There *is* a correct way to pack a book securely and soundly, but it takes time, effort, and materials to do so. The basic idea here is to isolate the book from damage as completely as possible without casting it in Lucite. Put simply, it shouldn't rattle around inside whatever enclosure you've placed it in to mail it. This is surprisingly easy to do, but as I said, it requires attention and effort to do it correctly.

Let me give you a list of supplies you'll need if you're at all serious about this thing: wrapping paper (plain; can be butcher paper, freezer paper, or unused newsprint), corrugated cardboard, bubble wrap, cardboard boxes/mailers, padded mailers (bubble, not shredded paper), packing tape, glue (yes, glue), polystyrene peanuts, and some place to keep it all.

Quite a list, right? I use all of these at one time or another, and most of them all the time. If you order things from Amazon, or get packages in the mail either from retail catalogs or online venues, a lot of this can be scavenged and recycled. Ask your friends; most of the time they throw whatever they get away, and I'm sure they'd be delighted to pass it along to you.

> *Paper:* Sometimes white butcher/freezer paper comes as box stuffing. It isn't terribly good for that, but some companies use it, and it can be flattened out. Also, if you look sharp, you can frequently get roll-ends of unprinted newsprint from job-printers or newspapers; as long as it's clean, it's perfectly appropriate to wrap books in. Do not use it to fill in a box, though, since crumpled paper will respond to rough handling by compressing rather than by expanding, and bang goes your isolation.

> *Cardboard:* Any good, clean box that comes your way and is too big to actually ship a book or two in is fodder for packing material. Use a sharp knife, and carefully cut the box along the folds into flat panels. Make your cuts as straight as you can; that will help you later.

> *Bubble wrap:* If you get a supply of this wonderful stuff sufficient to your needs without having to lay out cash for it, let me know how you did it. Most of what comes my way is torn or in pieces too small to be used effectively, or is covered in tape. I buy it in 12 inch x 350 foot rolls, perforated at 1 foot intervals, in the 3/16 inch bubble size. You'd be surprised how quickly one of these rolls goes, too, especially if you're running auctions every week. And the boxes break down into really, really nice big panels.

Boxes/mailers: Smaller boxes that come from Amazon or B&N or the like are just as perfect for sending *your* books as they were for sending *theirs*. If you have a space problem, break them down flat or nest them.

Padded mailers: Find the best price you can, and buy as many as you can. Used mailers, if opened carefully, can be easily reused. Don't buy the ones that are padded with shredded paper, since you're going to have to perform a little minor surgery in order to achieve that isolation I've been talking about and you don't want that stuff leaking all over the place. I use mostly the #4 and #5 sizes, with an occasional #00 for the small stuff.

Packing tape: No way around it, you gotta buy it. I recommend the 2" rolls with a self-contained cutter. I use the clearest tape I can find, but that's just a matter of taste unless you plan to use it to secure address labels, in which case it's mandatory. You're going to use a lot of it, too.

Glue: Elmer's, or any other white glue. You won't need anything stronger.

Peanuts: You should be able to get all of these you'll ever need from friends and family. In all the years I've done this, I've never bought a single one. Store them in trash bags.

A place for it all: I keep most of my supplies in a box I can shove under a table out of the way. The right box will hold cardboard flats, folded wrapping paper, padded mailers in various sizes, manila envelopes (yes, I do use them, but only in very specialized cases), a roll or two of tape, an 18" ruler, and a few other things I can cram into a corner without bending or breaking anything else. When I'm not packing books, it sits quietly all by itself and doesn't get in the way, and when I need it, it's right there where I can get to it.

Something else you can recycle to keep your books safe are pressed-paper egg cartons and drink carriers, as long as they're clean and dry. After all, why not use that most common—not to mention lightest—of packing materials, air? Both items can be set in the bottom of a box so that the books are kept away from possible sharp objects or just the bumps and bruises that boxes in transit are heir to. These things otherwise get thrown away after a single use; if they're usable (and if clean they certainly are), why not add them to your arsenal of immobilization? It will help you cut costs, and anything that does that increases your profits.

Of course, you'll also need a sharp knife and a straightedge, but that goes without saying, right? Please tell me it does.

The first thing I do is to wrap the book in paper. Please note that I am not talking about newspaper here, but clean butcher/freezer paper or unprinted newsprint. Wrapping a book in newspaper almost guarantees the transfer of ink to the book, and there goes at least one condition grade. Make sure you wrap the book tightly but without warping the book in the process. This will protect the book from any dust or soil on the cardboard.

Next comes the cardboard flat. Cut it to fit the height of the book, then lay the book on the flat so that the spine edge is parallel with the left edge of the flat. With a pencil, mark where the far right edge of the book is on the flat. Draw a straight line with a ruler from top to bottom, then carefully score—don't cut—that line. This is your first fold. You may have to use two smaller flats to cover the book completely.

Repeat this until you've wrapped the book in the cardboard, almost like a slipcase. This is the first real layer of protection against the slings and arrows of modern shipping procedures and handling. Don't quibble, it's necessary. I could tell you stories about the way some morons send books that would curl your mother's hair. I've gotten boxes stuffed so full of unwrapped books that the seams had split to the point that books were ready to fall out. Had they spent another day in the care of the delivery service, it would have been a dead loss.

At this point, if you've cut your flat to the right size to begin with[9], you should have an overlap. How big an overlap depends on how big the flat was originally, as well as the thickness of the book, but if you've done your job right, you got a flap of cardboard. Take some white glue, and apply it to the flap, making damned sure that you haven't put on so much that it will squeeze out and adhere to the book. That way lies madness and a dissatisfied customer. Hold the flap down until the glue sets. This should only take a few minutes; if you get bored, just put a heavy weight on top to hold it in place.

Next comes the bubble wrap. The stuff I use comes perforated at 12" intervals, so unroll three squares and tear it off as one piece. Fold it in half lengthways, and with a knife or scissors cut along the fold. This will give you two 18" pieces, one of which is sufficient for most standard hardcovers and trade paperbacks. Wrap the book in the bubble wrap, same as you did with the paper.

What you now have is a book protected by paper against soiling, and against rough handling by cardboard and padded wrapping. You have, in essence, an armored book. If you've done it right, your customer can work their way through the bubbles and simply slide the book out of the cardboard. You've done your job right the way down the line by delivering their purchase to them in the same condition in which it left your hands. Believe me, they'll appreciate it and come back for more.

But you aren't done yet. Many booksellers eschew padded bags, and, considering how most yobbos use them I can't say that they're wrong. But there is a right way to use them, one that will complete the process you began with the clean paper.

First, choose an appropriately sized mailer. Too much mailer will make your job more difficult, and is a waste of resources; too small and the book won't fit in the first place. If you have previously used, but clean and intact mailers, then by all mean use them before breaking open a pack you've paid money for. Insert the wrapped book in the mailer. You're going to have some extra space, and your task now is to make sure that the book you just spent time and effort in protecting against Bluto the UPS Guy doesn't spend the next week shifting around inside the mailer and possibly succumbing to being tossed around like a Frisbee at a Doobie Brothers concert.

Here's how you deal with that extra space, and how you ensure that your book is as isolated against handling as is possible:

- With scissors or a knife, cut down both sides of the mailer to just above the top of the book. You now have a flap that you can tuck inside over the top of the book and down behind it. I find that tucking is easier if I cut a wedge on both sides, but your mileage may vary.

- Tuck the rear flap over and behind the book snugly, then fold the front flap over that and use the adhesive strip to seal the package. You have now added yet another layer of padding to the mix; if you've followed directions, you could play soccer with this thing and it won't let the book get damaged. If the package is tight, nothing inside it will move, and that's 90% of it right there.

Of course, there are going to be times when a box is preferable to a padded mailer, so here's how you do that:

- Wrap the book as described, and then choose a box not too much larger than the book (or books) you're sending.

- Make sure the seams are tight (I routinely re-tape every box I use), and if necessary, use egg cartons or drink carriers (as described above) to pad the bottom.

- Place the wrapped book in, then fill in any and all empty space with peanuts or something equally light and bulky.[10]

- Shake the box before sealing it. If you can hear any movement inside, you need to add more.

That's pretty much it. If you follow the above principles, or at the very least use them as a guide to devise your own process, your customers should receive their books in the same condition in which they left, no matter how roughly they're handled in between.

11

Ready To Go

There you have it. I hope I've given you a leg up towards being a bookseller, however small or big an operator you want to be. I hope that this little book has been informative, instructional, and inspirational. I'm sure I've left stuff out, but with luck we'll update from time to time. If you have questions or comments, or if you want to tell me about your own experiences as an avocational bookseller, write the publisher at the address in the front of the book. Who knows? You just may make it possible for me to add a chapter.

Good luck and great hunting!

Notes

1. Let's be clear about this. You aren't going to make a living from it, but if you do it right you'll be able to put some money in the bank. This is a "hobby" the way some elaborate and expensive model train layouts are a "hobby"—one that takes a lot more time and effort and money than just collecting commemorative spoons. To me, that makes it an avocation, something that involves mare attention than just racking your latest acquisition.

2. Nah, let's do it now: a table cover for each table you intend to rent, pen and paper, a pocket calculator, some sort of bookends (I use the thin, bent-metal ones used in libraries) and/or book easels, business cards and/or bookmarks, change (plenty of singles and fives), bags (recycling plastic grocery bags works well), and a hand-cart. Mine converts to a dolly in about two seconds, and makes a huge difference when loading and unloading the car—you don't have to wait for a hotel luggage cart. A small bottle of hand sanitizer is a necessity, since you're going to be handling money and handing books to customers; a case of the con-crud is bad enough without (literally) handing it off to your buyers. Sanitizer goes a long way to preventing that. Use it often and offer it to your fellow hucksters.

3.   It was all Mary's idea, by the way. I'd been transporting my stock in big boxes, then unpacking them onto the table and trying desperately to keep them in order and upright. She used the plastic boxes to store fabric, and with a little experimentation and adaptation, we discovered they worked perfectly for my purposes.

4   Please note that I use those terms advisedly. You can't hope to start right at the top, and you're going to learn as you go along. List the books, pay careful attention to details about condition, price them well, and you've got a serviceable catalog, even if it's only a few pages long. We can't all be Barry Levin or Lloyd Currey.

5   To a point. If they keep sending books back with niggling little complaints, just drop them from your mailing list. You may be ethically obligated to satisfy them, but you're under no obligation whatsoever to sell to them at all if they keep complaining about minutiae.

6   Please do *not* bust my chops over my use of this fine old faanish term. It has a long and proud history in the annals of convention fandom, and was never intended in any way other than as good-natured ribbing, much like "filthy pro." Get over it.

7   With, of course, William Wu on first, Leslie What on second, and Ida Noe on third. Okay, I made that last one up.

8   Oh, all right. If you get a table or two in the dealers' room at a WorldCon, nobody is going to complain if you up your prices. After all, your expenses are going to be that much more, and if you don't cover them there's little point in being a dealer there in the first place. Add 20-25% and you should still come in under many of the other sellers in the room, and if you're higher, you can always offer the buyer a deal.

9   If you haven't, you'll have to use two smaller flats; that's okay, though, because not only do you really need that protection, but you can recycle two pieces of cardboard instead of just one.

10   Hey, you can use almost anything to fill in that space. My Significant Other used to quilt, and a lot of batting scraps made their way into my supply box. Batting is light, and will add yet another layer of protection.

Appendix

Specialty booksellers

This list is necessarily incomplete, but these are some of the sellers I've dealt with successfully over the years, and whose expertise is most trustworthy. They're in no particular order.

Nicholas J. Certo
P. O. Box 10305
Newburgh, NY
12552-0305

Ziesing Books
P. O. Box 76
Shingletown, CA 96008
(530) 474-1580

Graham Holroyd, Books
31 Lancer Place
Webster, NY 14580
585-670-9846
gholroyd@rochester.rr.com
http://www.booksareeverything.com/

Book It, Inc.
Grant Thiessen
P.O. Box 1
Neche, ND U.S.A. 58265
204-324-8548 Fax 204-324-1628
http://www.bookitinc.com/

L. W. Currey, Inc.
P.O. Box 187
203 Water Street
Elizabethtown, NY 12932-0187
Phone (518) 873-6477 - Fax (518) 873-9105
lloyd@lwcurrey.com
http://www.lwcurrey.com/

Barry R. Levin
720 Santa Monica Blvd.
Santa Monica, CA 90401
310-458-6111 Fax : 310-899-9404
http://www.raresf.com/bhome.html

Here is one of the most useful resources you'll find. It's the **Antiquarian Booksellers' Association of America** website, and it's rife with important information that you're going to need in order to be a reliable and trustworthy bookman, even if it *is* only as a hobby: http://www.abaa.org/

In particular, the link "Learn More About Rare Books" will give you practically everything you need in the way of terminology and other bibliophilic particulars, so have at it.

About the Author

Bud Webster has been buying and selling sf and fantasy for almost 40 years, beginning with comics and soon graduating to real books, the ones that have more words than pictures. Most of his working career has been spent in retail of one sort or another, and his bookselling experience ranges from large book store chains to independent specialty bookshops.

Over the years, Bud's supplemented his hard-won knowledge of the field by poring over his personal reference library and by consulting those even more obsessed than he. Along the way he also proved he paid attention while reading all of those books by selling fiction and nonfiction to a variety of markets including *Analog* and *The Magazine of Fantasy and Science Fiction*.

Bud's one of few living Americans who can properly be called an award-winning epic poet. He lives in sin in Central Virginia with an understanding woman and three furiously neurotic damn cats (aren't they all?).

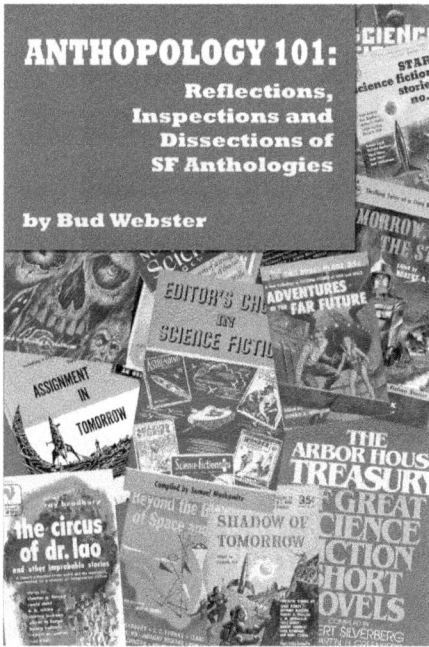

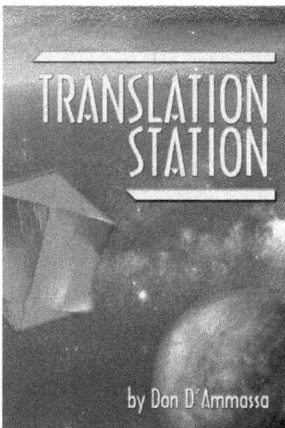

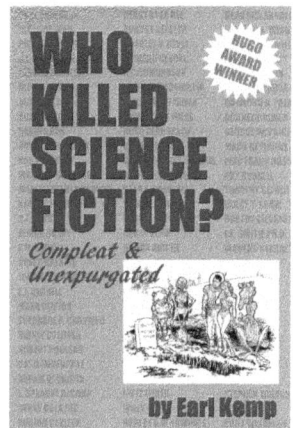

www.ingramcontent.com/pod-product-compliance
Lightning Source LLC
Chambersburg PA
CBHW060408050426
42449CB00009B/1938